COLLEGE ADMISSIONS
without the Crazy

NANCY DONEHOWER, Ph.D.

© 2014 by Nancy Donehower

All rights reserved. No part of this publication may be reproduced or distributed in any form or by any means, or stored in a database or retrieval system, without the prior written permission of the publisher.

ISBN: 978-0-9862362-1-1

*To students embarking on the road to college:
I wish you an enlightening journey and every success
when you reach your destination.*

Contents

Foreword	9
1. It's a Jungle Out There	13
2. Understanding Where Crazy Comes From	17
3. Set Your Starting Point	23
4. Gather and Evaluate Information Effectively	35
5. Don't Sabotage Your Decision Process	49
6. More about Making Good Decisions	61
7. For Parents	69
Acknowledgments	77
Appendix 1: Questionnaire	79
Appendix 2: Resources	83
About the Author	85

Foreword

It happened again on a recent flight. In a casual conversation with my seatmate, I was asked what I do for a living. I replied, "I'm a college counselor. I help students apply to college."

My seatmate offered a sympathetic nod of the head and the comment, "You must deal with a lot of nervous students and parents."

This is one of the three most common responses I receive when I tell people what I do for a living. For the record, the other two most common responses are, "Huh. You know, I went to _____, but I'd never get in if I applied there today," and "This is great: can you tell me if my daughter/son/cousin/grandchild/friend will get into _____?"

No one ever just smiles politely and turns away. Everyone has opinions and questions about the college admissions process, regardless of whether they are related to a high school junior or senior. This has been true throughout the three decades I have been working in the admissions field.

The college admissions process has a real grip on our cultural consciousness, and the level of hype, anxiety, and stress around it appear to be at an all-time high. As one high school senior said to me, "Everyone is freaking out about this."

It doesn't have to be that way. It is admittedly hard to turn down the noise surrounding the college admissions frenzy, but this book offers the tools to help students do just that.

College Admissions Without the Crazy draws on my training as a psychologist and my broad and deep experience in college admissions to offer a new approach to the admissions process. I combine time-tested strategies with insights from the social sciences to guide students through the challenges they face as they begin to look at colleges, work on applications, and weigh offers of admission.

I wrote this book to help high school students and their parents understand the social, developmental, and technological context in which the college admissions process takes place. I believe that understanding the larger context will help you recognize and avoid the underlying causes of stress and frustration that can scuttle the whole enterprise.

But, you say, *the shelves (electronic and traditional) are filled with books offering college admissions advice. How is this book different?*

It's different because this isn't a traditional how-to guide for the admissions process. Those guides are task oriented and tell you, for example, how to make a college application timeline, or write a personal résumé, or craft a compelling essay.

This book is student oriented. It helps you understand why you may feel overwhelmed or just plain stuck as you approach the various tasks of the college admissions process—and then it offers the tools and detailed advice you need to get unstuck.

This book is also different because my experience within and perspective on the field of college admissions is unique.

Thirty years ago, I entered the field of college admissions after earning a Ph.D. in psychology. Over the course of my career, I have developed a 360-degree view of the admissions process: as the dean of admissions, I had the final say about which students to admit, waitlist, or deny. As the director of college counseling at academically challenging college-preparatory high schools and as a college consultant, I have guided students from the United States and abroad as they searched for and applied to colleges.

My background and training have led me to view the admissions process not only as a sequence of tasks to be accomplished according to a specific timeline but also as an important learning opportunity and developmental milestone for teenagers. My insights about both can help you build a firm foundation for success in the admissions process.

I know that the road to college is not notably clear or easy to navigate for a variety of reasons. I want you to think of this book as the equivalent of night-vision goggles for the college admissions process. It's the book you read *before* things get underway, so that you can see the terrain clearly and avoid potential hazards along the way.

"Well begun is half done," as Aristotle said. It is my hope that this book will help you begin well, by providing context and a perspective on the admissions process that help you understand it more thoroughly. Armed with that knowledge, you can work through each phase more effectively.

1
It's a Jungle Out There

College admissions, an annual rite of passage for students, is a source of stress and pressure for many. It has been so for several decades.

Over the course of my thirty-year career in college admissions, I have witnessed major transformations in the field. I have seen an increase in the levels of stress, anxiety, and panic-driven behavior it produces in high school students and their parents.

The process of selecting, applying to, and deciding which college to attend receives vastly more media attention now than ever before. What used to be a relatively private rite of passage is now an ongoing focus for the media and a subject of community scrutiny, compounding the stress and confusion many teenagers already feel as high school draws to a close. In addition, technology has altered every aspect of the admissions process.

COLLEGE ADMISSIONS Without the Crazy

Technology has changed the type and amount of information available about colleges, it has changed the ways students access this information, and it has changed the ways that students produce, submit, and monitor the status of their applications—and eventually receive their admissions decisions.

These changes in the admissions process have increased the challenges students face as they search for and apply to colleges. Students tell me they feel overwhelmed by the prospect of finding and applying to colleges that will suit them. I also see that they spend a lot of time and effort chasing information that is ultimately unnecessary or unhelpful and that they agonize about the decisions they must make.

For sure, there is a lot about the college admissions process that can make you crazy. But to those who amplify the stress, I say, "Sell crazy someplace else. We're all stocked up here." (OK, I borrowed those lines from the 1997 film *As Good as It Gets*. Thank you, Mark Andrus and James L. Brooks, who wrote the screenplay.)

I believe there is a better way to approach the college admissions process. I believe it's possible to hang on to your sanity and not be blown off course by all the hype and frenzy surrounding the process.

The key is to focus on the fundamentals: pay attention to the essential steps involved in finding, applying to, and selecting a college to attend.

That's what this book is about.

What Lies Ahead:
- **Chapter 2** is addressed to students and parents. It discusses in detail the factors that combine to make the college admissions world so crazy these days. It also lays out the essential—but often overlooked—steps students should take to maximize their chances of success.

- **Chapters 3 through 6** are directed specifically to students. These chapters explain each of the essential steps in detail. The format is the same in each chapter: I start with an overview of the task and then discuss the potential pitfalls that can obstruct your progress at this stage. After that, I show you how to avoid those pitfalls, and offer a practical plan of action.
- **Chapter 7** is for parents. It discusses the challenges parents face as their children navigate the admissions process and shares the strategies of families who have managed the process successfully.
- In the **Appendices,** you will find a questionnaire for students and a list of useful resources.

Inevitably, there will be some bumps along the road to college, but if you follow the time-tested advice in this book, you will minimize those bumps and lower your stress. The college admissions process is challenging, to be sure, but it doesn't have to be a sanity-sucking nightmare. Trust me on this and read on.

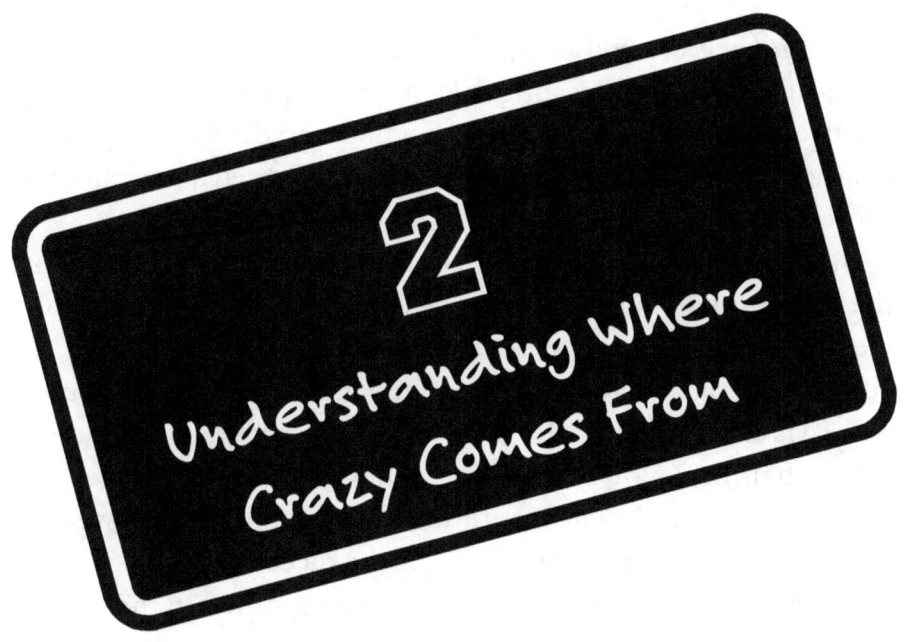

2. Understanding Where Crazy Comes From

Over the last three decades, several factors have combined to make a significant impact on the college admissions process. Among the most important are: the growth of secondary sources of information about colleges, the impact of technology on the process, and the increasingly global nature of the applicant pools at US colleges and universities.

Let's take a closer look at how these factors and other influences have ramped up the craziness in the college admissions process.

What Causes Crazy: Part I

The world of college admissions is varied and complicated. The elements that make it so fall into two categories: the general, which is more enduring, and the specific, which changes with the times. Let's look at the general factors first.

College *has both literal and symbolic meanings in our society.* Literally, college is a place for educating students, a place where they develop intellectual and personal skills they will use in the working world. On the other hand, college is also widely regarded as a symbol of success and status.

In their symbolic role, colleges have morphed into brands, and the colleges and universities that have emerged as premium brands are highly sought after because, along with celebrity and the accumulation of material wealth, attendance at a premium-brand college is an important hallmark of personal success in our society.

The hallmarks of success for colleges and universities are similar: premium-brand institutions have the luxury of wealth, via large endowments and consistently successful fund-raising; they have celebrity, which means name recognition in the United States and abroad; and they are highly selective, turning away a large percentage of applicants each year.

We love quest and competition narratives. From Homer's *Odyssey* to *The Hunger Games* (not to mention many reality TV shows), we find heroic journeys and contests uniquely compelling. The college admissions process plays right into this, as each year a new group of students enters the arena to undertake the quest for admission. The competition for college admission has particular resonance in our culture because it is such an important signifier of success and status. This is a high-stakes competition.

The uncertainty and unpredictability of the outcomes of each student's quest for admission heighten the tension of the competition. Where the prize (in this case, admission to one of the three dozen or so most highly selective colleges) is desperately coveted and the risk of failure is great (85 percent or more of the applicants are turned away from these schools), we may resort to unusual or superstitious behaviors in our attempts to reduce uncertainty and manage this risk.

Many potent developmental and familial issues converge around the college admissions process. There is a lot of emotional and psychological freight that accompanies the admissions process. In addition to the academic and personal pressures that can accompany their senior year, students are working through issues of independence and self-determination as well as the prospect of moving away from home and family. Parents, watching their children take these steps toward separation, are anxious and want to minimize the possibilities that their children will face disappointment or outright failure. Many moms and dads also see college admissions results as a kind of report card on their parenting. They are as eager for those A's (admission offers) as their children. And let's not leave out the stress caused by the financial side of things. The cost of college creates many issues and burdens for families as well.

So right out of the gate, before any college visits are made or application forms filled out, there are general factors that make the admissions process challenging.

What Causes Crazy: Part II

General issues are just part of the picture, though. The following specific factors increase the craziness of the college admissions process and take it to a new level in the twenty-first century.

Demographics make a difference. The number of high school graduates in the United States remains high, and because many colleges and universities have expanded their recruitment efforts and now seek students from all around the world, competition for space in the entering classes at many colleges has increased significantly. The fact that students commonly apply to more colleges than they did in previous years means the applicant pools at many institutions are filled with even more hopeful students. Application numbers are up, and where colleges have not increased the size of their entering classes, admission rates are down.

Too many people believe the myth that there is only a small group of "good" colleges out there. We have a cultural tendency to equate institutional popularity and selectivity with quality. That tendency combines with our affection for rankings and ratings provided by college guides to create a false sense of the scarcity of "good colleges." That false sense of scarcity further amplifies the competitive craziness of the college admissions process.

There's a glut of information and "experts" offering advice and opinion about colleges and the admission process. As previously mentioned, over the last few decades, colleges expanded their recruitment efforts and used technology to reach out to prospective applicants around the world. At the same time, the amount of information about colleges available to prospective students increased dramatically as media outlets seized on admissions as a hot topic and hundreds if not thousands of websites offering all types of information, advice, and rumors about colleges and the admissions process emerged.

Students applying to college now must sift through exponentially more information than students applying to college five or more years ago. As a result, many "experts" have appeared, offering to help students filter and make sense of the tsunami of information that engulfs them. In the education field as in all others, though, all experts are not created equal. I am especially intrigued by the rise of what I call the "citizen counselor." These are individuals who don't have a lot of experience with the admissions process but who are able to sell their advice and opinions nonetheless.

We've made the private public. College preferences, hopes, and choices have been primary topics of conversation for high school students and their parents for decades. It used to be easier to keep a lid on your personal information, though. Now, with social media tools like Instagram, Twitter, and Facebook changing the meaning of personal privacy, a student's hopes and plans for college can be broadcast widely, quickly, and without the student's knowledge.

The ease with which information about an individual's college admissions process can be shared—and the speed and range with which anxieties, rumors, and wild untruths about the admissions process can spread—ramp up the craziness of the process.

How to Keep Crazy in Its Place
There is a way to maintain your sanity, keep a sense of perspective, and navigate this process with reduced stress.

In coming chapters, I will explain how to lay a firm foundation for success as you research and apply to colleges and as you choose a college to attend. My approach makes use of insights from the social sciences, neuroscience, and my own years of experience in the admissions field to guide you through the admissions process, avoiding things that might trip you up or freak you out along the way. I will help you turn down the noise that surrounds college admissions so you can hear your own voice clearly and let it guide you to a satisfying outcome.

What are the three essential steps in the college admissions process? In a nutshell, they are:

1. Set your starting point.
2. Gather and evaluate information effectively.
3. Don't sabotage your decision process.

There is a better way to work through the college admissions process. If you are willing to invest time and thought at the outset, you'll build a firm foundation for success—and lower your stress levels too. Let's get started!

3
Set Your Starting Point

When I begin to work with students, my first questions are: How are you feeling about the college admissions process? Do you have questions or concerns as you look ahead? The quotes below are a representative sample of the responses I've received over the years:

"I'm concerned about not knowing which colleges to look at, or if I even want to go to college."

"I don't know when I will ever have time to write college applications, and I have no idea where to apply or even what I'm looking for in a school."

"How do I know what I want? How am I supposed to choose the right college?"

"I'm concerned about my parents' ideas about college because they stress me out. I'm worried that I won't know what college is right for me, and that my parents might not like my choice."

"What if I find the perfect college and don't get in?"

Do any of those responses seem familiar to you? If so, you're in good company. The majority of students I've worked with have had some worries about the admissions process and its outcomes. If you're feeling nervous, this chapter will help you understand the source of some of those feelings and then help you move beyond them and get off to a good start with the admissions process.

Others of you may not feel worried at all. If that's the case, it's great that you are not stressing over things and are ready to jump right in. You may be able to zip right through the first part of this chapter and go right to the section that helps you set your starting point. If you have friends who are feeling nervous about the admissions process, though, reading the first part of the chapter will help you understand where some of their worries come from.

No matter how you feel, it will be helpful to focus your thoughts and take time for self-reflection so you can set your starting point. This is the most important thing you can do to make the process go smoothly. After all, if you don't know where you're starting from, it's harder to get where you're going.

What's Ahead
This chapter talks about the factors that make it hard to determine your starting point and explains the obstacles you may encounter as you begin. From there, we'll move to a series of questions for you to answer. These answers will help you get a fix on your

preferences and help bring your starting point into view. Once you've got that starting point, we'll briefly discuss how to translate those preferences into an initial list of colleges to research.

First, let's look at the issues that make it difficult to get started.

What Are the Obstacles?

While each person is different, I have found that similar issues affect most students as they start the college admissions process. These are:

Future Shock

Up till now, your life has been anchored in the present. You think about what's going on at school, with your family, and with your immediate circle of friends and activities. You haven't really had to think much about the future in a very specific way. And most likely, the world of college is largely unknown to you, though if you have an older sibling or friends already in college, you may have a general idea of what life in college is like.

It can be difficult to look ahead and difficult to imagine yourself in a new environment. In addition, for most students, the junior and senior years of high school are busy and pressured. There are lots of demands on your time and attention, and the future takes a back seat to the present. Some of you may feel that college might not be the right choice for you and want to look at other options, though you might not be sure what those options are. Or you may think that you'd like to go to college, just not right after high school. You might want to get off the conveyor belt of school, school, and more school for a year or two and then think about next steps.

Whatever your thoughts as you near the end of high school, one thing is inescapable: like winter in *Game of Thrones*, the future is coming.

Test Anxiety

If you read this and immediately thought about the SAT and ACT, you're not alone. Surprise! Those tests aren't what I'm talking about here.

For most students, the challenges and choices of the college admissions process feel like the first big test of adulthood. This test—the process of making those choices—carries a lot of anxiety for many students.

Previously, many decisions were made for you, or the consequences of decisions you made weren't life altering. (Soccer or basketball? Regular English or AP? Stick with debate club or try something new?) Now, though, the stakes have changed, and you may feel that if you make the wrong choice or if you don't get into the college of your dreams, it's game over.

And if that isn't enough, here's another tricky aspect of test anxiety: even if you don't feel especially anxious about the future, chances are that your parents are very concerned about it on your behalf. They love you and want to see you do well, so they are experiencing their own test anxiety as you approach this important decision point in your life. Sometimes, dealing with their anxiety can be more difficult than dealing with your own.

Sudden-onset Celebrity

You may notice this first in the summer between the sophomore and junior year of high school, or maybe it will crop up a little later. First the people in your immediate circle of family and friends start to ask where you want to go to college. Then the circle widens, and by the time you're a senior, it seems as though everyone in the world wants to know your college plans. And then they want to give you their opinions about your choices. This is partly because asking you about your plans is their way of connecting with the big story that college admissions has become these days and partly because asking a high school junior or senior about college plans is pretty much a conversational reflex. Whatever the cause, it's difficult to escape the college spotlight. Dealing with all this outside interest in your plans for the future is challenging, especially when you're in the process of figuring things out for yourself.

Group Dynamics
Humans are social animals. As a species, we like to communicate, and we like to connect with others. That's one reason why social media tools are so popular.

Take a minute and think about the various groups you belong to. You're part of a family, so that's one group. You go to a particular school—that's another. You may be part of a youth group, a sports team, and one or more clubs—still more groups! And when you "like" something or someone online, you're part of that fan group too. That's all great—until you run into groupthink.

Are you familiar with this already? *Groupthink* is a term social psychologists use to describe the way that people in groups work toward consensus, often setting aside their individual opinions or priorities. There's lots of interesting research about the power that a group can exert over an individual. For example, when a group reaches a conclusion, an individual in that group may be reluctant to disagree, preferring to maintain harmony within the group. Research also shows that there's strength in numbers. When many people hold the same opinion, it can make an individual second-guess his or her own conclusion. This can be a real problem as you are considering colleges. If you like a place that others in any of your groups aren't familiar with or tend not to like, it can be tempting to cross that college off your list and substitute the group's judgment for your own.

Can't Hear Your Own Voice

When it comes to choosing colleges, many students do substitute group opinions for their own, at least initially. Sometimes they do this to maintain harmony within a group. For example, you may not want to disappoint family members by not applying to a college they think is perfect for you. Sometimes it's because you think you're pretty similar to a person or group of people who chose a particular college, and you think that if it worked for them, it will work for you. A lot of the time, though, you'll substitute outside opinions for your own because you haven't been able to figure out what you really think. What with all the advice and opinions out there, you can't hear your own voice, and like the students quoted at the beginning of this chapter, you aren't sure where to begin or what you should keep in mind as you try to make up your own mind.

Getting Past These Obstacles

All of these issues make the college admissions process seem pretty daunting. At this point you may feel like you want to run away and hide. Actually, that's not the worst idea! OK, not the running away part, but you are going to need some space and quiet so you can hear your own thoughts and figure out what is most important to you. Let's get started on that.

First of all, relax. I know that is easier said than done, but once you break this process down into small parts, it is very manageable. Keep these points in mind as you move ahead:

You are not shooting at a very small target from a very great distance. If you think there is one "perfect" college out there for you and your life will be over if you don't find it, all I can say is (and I mean this in the nicest possible way) *get over it*. There are many colleges that will be great matches for you. Keep reading, and you'll be on the path to finding them.

"Fantasy floods in where fact leaves a vacuum."
I borrowed this line from Peter Shaffer's play *Lettice and Lovage* because it is so relevant to the college admissions process. I've mentioned before that there is a lot of rumor and hype out there about how difficult the college admissions process is. This is why many students start the process thinking that they won't be able to manage it and that they won't get in anywhere. When you're entirely new to the process, you don't have a lot of factual knowledge to rely on, so you're at the mercy of the rumors and hype. But when you actually start your research and gather information, you will see that the process isn't as overwhelming as you may have imagined.

"Just take it bird by bird."
Here's the backstory on this quote, from writer Anne Lamott: "Thirty years ago my older brother, who was ten years old at the time, was trying to get a report on birds written that he'd had three months to write. It was due the next day. We were out at our family cabin in Bolinas, and he was at the kitchen table close to tears, surrounded by binder paper and pencils and unopened books on birds, immobilized by the hugeness of the task ahead. Then my father sat down beside him, put his arm around my brother's shoulder, and said, 'Bird by bird, buddy. Just take it bird by bird.'"

Though Lamott offered this anecdote as advice to would-be writers, it is excellent advice for you as you enter the college admissions process. Take things one step at a time. Don't make yourself crazy by thinking about *everything* that you have to do. Stay focused on each particular task and you'll get there.

You know more about what you're looking for than you think you do.
You've had lots of experiences already that have helped you define preferences and make choices. Now you need to reflect on those

preferences and choices and apply that knowledge to this new context of college admissions.

Are you ready to start? Skip over to Appendix 1, where I have included a questionnaire for you to complete. You will use these responses to set your starting point and come up with your own personal yardstick so you can see how different colleges measure up to your preferences. When you're finished, come back here, and we will look at the next steps.

Building a List of Colleges to Investigate

Once you have gathered information about yourself and your preferences, the next step is to translate those preferences into an initial list of colleges to investigate.

There are several ways to start. If you want a step-by-step guide for making a college list, have a look at my e-book, *Start Your College Search Without the Crazy*. This guide offers comprehensive advice for building a college list and shows you how one sample student created, focused, and finalized the list of colleges she applied to.

Alternately, you may get the ball rolling by using one of the many college search engines available online. The websites cappex.com and zinch.com have search engines many students find helpful. (These websites are also used as student recruitment and marketing tools by colleges.) The College Board also has a very user-friendly college search engine on its site: collegeboard.org. For those who like a lot of objective data to compare, the National Center for Education Statistics has a very good search engine too: nces.ed.gov/collegenavigator.

Be aware that college search engines can be both a miracle tool and a source of immense frustration. These search engines can help you cut through a lot of information quickly, but they can also give you results that are way off base.

What can you do to get the best results? I suggest that you use two or three college search engines to help you come up with an initial list of colleges.

As you do so, you will quickly discover that no two search engines ask their questions in exactly the same way. But don't worry about that: armed with your responses to the questionnaire included in this book, do your best to align those responses with the questions posed. Answer the questions about items that matter most to you. If you have no feeling either way about a particular item, it's OK to skip it.

Search engines are only one resource for you to use, however. You should also visit the college counselor in your high school to discuss your preferences and ask for suggestions. Talk with your favorite teachers too. Ask them what they think might be good college matches based on the items that are most important to you.

Once you have a few names on your list, you can make use of the *compare colleges* or *other colleges like this* feature that some college guides and search engines offer. Those recommendations can be helpful while you are in the early stages of building a list.

After completing these steps, you may have just a few colleges on your initial list or you may have lots—no problem either way. The important thing is that you can now get started with more serious research and see how the schools on your initial list match up with your starting point criteria. You're ready to move ahead to the next chapter, where we will look at how to gather and filter information about colleges.

Still Having Trouble Getting Started?

But wait, you say. You can't answer a lot of the questions I posed. You don't know what size of college might be best for you. You don't know what you want to study, and you don't feel like you can evaluate a campus atmosphere because you have never been on a college campus. So you don't really have preferences you feel confident about, and you can't find a place to get started.

Not a problem.

If, like some students, you don't feel you know enough yet to set preferences and make some initial choices, then you can approach the college search process from a different angle. You won't escape the questionnaire, though. I will ask you to return to it later.

To get things underway, go and spend some time on college campuses of different types that are close to where you live. Don't miss a lot of your high school classes in order to do this, however! In my part of the country—Portland, Oregon—students are fortunate that they don't have to travel far in order to visit smaller liberal arts and sciences colleges; medium, large, and very large public universities; colleges with specialized programs and curricula; and colleges with different religious affiliations. They can visit schools with urban, suburban, and rural-feeling campuses.

When students I work with have difficulty figuring out what is most important to them, I ask them to pick out three or four institutions in the area that are very different from one another and spend half a day on each campus. Any group of colleges will do, as long as the colleges they visit differ from one another in size, location, and atmosphere. This never fails. Once students have a chance to see themselves in different college settings, preferences instantly emerge. And as preferences emerge, it is easier to complete the questionnaire.

As you continue, remember that your starting point is not necessarily going to be your ending point. As you do your research and learn about colleges, your opinions and priorities may change. Let them! A lot happens between the winter or spring of junior year, when most high school students begin the college search, and the fall of senior year, when you make final choices about colleges to apply to. Your priorities may change right up until the time you make a final decision about which college to attend. This is perfectly normal.

It's hard to appreciate this right now, but you have to have faith in the process. You have made a great beginning by taking the time for self-reflection and thinking about the factors that combine to make your starting point. Your task from here on out, in the words of a college professor I know, is to maintain the courage of your conviction and to maintain the courage of your confusion. In other words, trust what you know but don't be daunted by what you don't know. Trust the process.

Second, now that you have your starting point, it is fine and in fact desirable to discuss your priorities with others. However, you will want to manage the amount of time you spend discussing your search with family, friends, and your online communities. Seeking some amount of feedback and advice is fine. Obsessing over colleges and relentlessly judging and comparing your opinions with those of others is not.

In my experience, it becomes harder to maintain the privacy of your college search once you become a senior in high school, when college information becomes a currency that is always in trade. Resist the impulse to talk about college all the time, for at least two reasons: First, more din equals more distraction. It's easier to get confused and to be thrown off course when you are constantly swapping information with others. Second, you need time to process your thoughts by yourself, without input from an audience. Remember my earlier comments about groupthink.

Looking Ahead

Congratulations! You've accomplished one big step in the process, and now you have a list of colleges that form the starting point for your research. You are ready to move ahead. In the next chapter, we will look closely at how to efficiently and effectively separate the reliable information from the opinions and rumors about colleges.

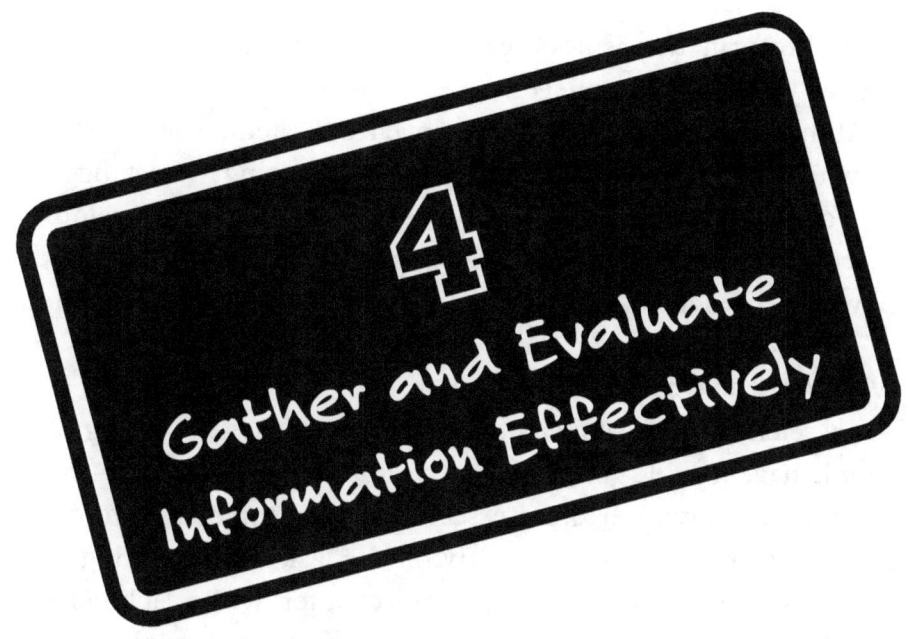

4
Gather and Evaluate Information Effectively

At this point, I'll assume that you have a preliminary list of colleges that seem interesting. You are now ready to settle down and begin your research.

The good news is, there is no shortage of information about colleges.

The bad news is, there is no shortage of information about colleges.

What's Ahead

Equipped with the initial list of colleges you have created, you will now learn how to efficiently and effectively investigate the colleges that interest you. In this chapter you will learn how to gather information and, more importantly, how to evaluate the information you collect. You will learn how to filter the data you collect so you don't waste time with information that is unnecessary, unreliable, or outright wrong. I'm sure you know already that all information is not created equal; you will see this in a *big* way as you research colleges.

At this point, you will begin to move from satellite view to street view for the colleges that interest you. You're going to start digging into details. In this stage of the process, your goal is to develop as thorough and accurate a picture of each college as you can to see how closely each college matches your preferences and priorities.

What Are the Obstacles?

Social scientists and data scientists could spend days explaining why people have trouble gathering and evaluating information—there is a ton of really interesting research on this topic. But we want to be very specific and focus only on the task of researching colleges. As I mentioned in the previous chapter, while each person is different, there are general issues that affect most people as they start to research colleges. These are:

Target: You
Right around your junior year in high school (and sometimes earlier), your plans for higher education become a source of intense interest for the many colleges that hope you will submit an application. You become the apple of their collective eye, the target of their attention.

The degree to which you are pursued by colleges may take you by surprise. It may not have occurred to you before, but for a variety of reasons, it is in every college's best interest to have as many applicants as possible each year. This is why colleges spend a lot of time and energy, not to mention big bucks, recruiting students to their applicant pools.

College admissions officers know that the biggest obstacle to success in building an applicant pool is just getting noticed. Maybe fifty colleges or so have the luxury of broad, national name recognition,

Gather and Evaluate Information Effectively

but *all* colleges work hard to build their applicant pools. So you will be the target of many—often quite sophisticated and personalized—marketing campaigns. Print and email communication is supplemented by Facebook pages, Twitter feeds, YouTube channels, and other means of outreach that colleges use to get your attention. Then there are the opportunities you have for personal contact: you can meet admissions representatives at college fairs, high school visits, and through interviews. Campus visits and "prospective student days" are also prime marketing opportunities that colleges hope will entice you to apply.

Most students enjoy the attention they get from colleges—at least at first! But while you're basking in the attention, do remain wary, because a valentine is not the same thing as a proposal of marriage. Courtship is not commitment.

While colleges are highly motivated to get you into their applicant pools, the fact that they work hard to recruit you is no guarantee of admission.

Well, duh, you say. *I know that.*

But you might be surprised at how often students (and parents) take these recruitment overtures more seriously than they are intended. I have seen this happen time and time again during my college counseling career. A student receives a personalized letter and is "invited" to apply to a college, or a "priority" application sent only to a "select group of students" drops into the electronic inbox, or a student has a friendly and optimistic exchange with an admissions officer, and concludes, *This is it! I'm in!*

I don't want to be a downer, but attaching too much significance to typical recruitment tactics is one of the most common mistakes that students make when evaluating college information. My advice: enjoy the attention you receive from colleges, but don't buy the sweatshirt until you have the actual offer of admission in hand.

COLLEGE ADMISSIONS Without the Crazy

(Caveat: The section above refers to recruitment overtures made to a majority of students. If you are a nationally ranked high school athlete, or if you have some other truly outstanding quality that a college or colleges crave, your recruitment process and the information you receive from colleges will be a bit different. All the same, wait for the formal offer of admission before you tell people where you're enrolling!)

Too Much Information (TMI) and the Two R's

The recruitment information produced by the colleges themselves is just the tip of the iceberg. If you didn't realize this already, you will quickly come to see that college admissions is an industry. There are countless guidebooks, myriad websites offering information about all aspects of college life, and a seemingly unending stream of blog posts, tweets, online forums, and articles in the media about colleges. And then there is all the information (whether you want it or not) you will receive from family, friends, your online community, teachers, counselors—and interested strangers. Some of this information is straightforward and factual, some if it is opinion, some of it is rumor. And there sure is a lot of it.

This glut of information can be paralyzing. You don't know where to begin, and you know there is absolutely no way that you will ever be able to look at all the resources, so you beat a retreat, try to block it out, and (suddenly, miraculously!) find that there is always something more pressing on your to-do list than college research.

Too much information (TMI) has stopped you in your tracks.

A common response to TMI is to look for shortcuts. This is entirely understandable—you've got a mountain of information in front of you, and you need to figure out some way to deal with it.

At this point you are apt to be led astray by the two Rs. The two Rs are insidious, because on the surface of things, they seem to

Gather and Evaluate Information Effectively

be such useful tools. *Rankings* and *Recommendations* both seem as though they will help you make sense of the glut of information about colleges, but in reality, these shortcuts can derail you. Bear with me here; I won't go into a lot of detail, but I do want to make a few points about the drawbacks of each R.

Rankings: A great deal has already been written about the drawbacks of various college rankings, and I don't want to go over that territory again. But here is the main problem, as I see it: any system that attempts to objectively rank an item of personal preference is inevitably flawed. The question of "best" in an absolute sense can never be resolved when individual taste or opinion is involved. It makes no more sense to ask, "What is the best college?" than it does to ask, "What is the best book ever written?" or "What is the best flavor of ice cream?"

Rankings can mislead you because they have a veneer of reliability. Often you can see at least some of the data that has been collected and compared to reach the proffered conclusions. *And rankings make it so easy to compare colleges!* you say.

The thing is, an institution's ranking has nothing at all to do with how satisfied you will be with the place, the people, or what you learn there.

A ranking is a data point that seems precise, but the appearance of precision masks the folly of the ranking exercise itself. Shortcuts that claim to lead you to the "best college" miss the point. You want to find the best colleges *for you*, so the only rankings that really matter are the ones you generate yourself.

Recommendations: We are all influenced by the opinions of others. We look at "likes," followers, and reviews regularly as we check out new places, products, and people. Recommendations can be useful shortcuts. If a close friend who shares your taste in movies tells you that you'll enjoy a film she really likes, chances are, you will. However, if you only use crowd-sourced reviews to figure out if you will enjoy a movie, your response will be less easy to predict. Why? The crowd doesn't know enough about you and your preferences to function as a useful predictor for you.

Before you object, I know that companies like Amazon and Netflix, for example, spend tons of money devising sophisticated algorithms that predict whether or not you'll like a new product, TV show, or movie. The difference is that you supply these companies with data about yourself through your purchases and/or your ratings, which allows them to filter products and recommend those they think you will like based on what you've already told them.

The same principle applies to recommendations you will receive about colleges. If a recommendation comes from someone who knows you, knows what you're looking for in a college, and has recent knowledge about the college they're recommending, then pay attention. This could be a valuable lead to follow.

On the other hand, if a recommendation comes from someone who lacks any one of those qualities, you'll need more information about the college before you rule it in or out as a possibility.

Be similarly vigilant when you make use of college reviews (another form of recommendation) to shortcut your information-gathering process. Opinions forcefully presented in any medium can be mistaken for facts, so consider the source when you're looking at reviews. Don't hesitate to ask yourself: Who is saying this, and why should I believe them?

This leads me to one more obstacle in your quest to gather accurate and reliable information about colleges.

Distinguishing Truth from Truthiness

Those of you who, like me, are devoted fans of Stephen Colbert will be familiar with the term *truthiness*, which he introduced in 2005.

Gather and Evaluate Information Effectively

Truthiness, he said, is "the truth you feel in your gut, regardless of what the facts support." "You can't prove truthiness with information," Colbert added, "you prove truthiness with more truthiness, in a process known as truthiness-iness" (*Colbert Report*, August 9, 2012).

When there is so much information available about colleges, and when opinion and attitude get as much (or more) attention than facts do, it is really easy to be sidetracked by truthiness. It gets even trickier when many people repeat something truthy about a college. Repetition increases the likelihood that an audience will mistake opinion for fact. So this whole issue of distinguishing truth from truthiness can be a real problem in the college search.

Getting Past These Obstacles

You face these obstacles of marketing, TMI, shortcuts, and distinguishing truth from truthiness every day as you make decisions about things like which brand of juice to buy, restaurant to try, movie to see, and song to download. You probably haven't worried very much about those obstacles before, however, because for most of you, your daily choices are pretty low stakes. When trying to figure out which colleges match your preferences and priorities, though, the stakes are higher, as we've discussed. You're on the verge of making a big investment of time and resources, and your decision could have potentially life-altering outcomes. I say this not to totally stress you out but to remind you that you are embarking on a serious task here—one that deserves your time and focused attention.

These steps will help you gather information efficiently and effectively and will help you develop your own set of filters as well.

Step One: Look for the Signal, Turn Down the Noise

As you research colleges, you will find that some information is useful: it comes from a reliable source, it fills in the picture you're creating of a particular college, and it helps you decide if the school is a match for your priorities. Other information you'll encounter will not be useful. When investigating further, you may find out that it was just rumor or that it was not relevant at all as you determine the match between your priorities and a college. Borrowing from the scientific world (and from Nate Silver's 2013 book, *The Signal and the Noise*), we'll call the useful and reliable information the signal and the unhelpful and unreliable information the noise. Your goal through the information-gathering phase is to focus on the signal and do your best to turn down the noise.

Differentiating between signal and noise will be difficult at first, but trust me: you will get better at it as you go along. Sure, you'll head down a few wrong paths at first and be distracted by appealingly presented noise, but that's OK. Once you're out there in the traffic of the college information universe, your ability to separate signal from noise will improve quickly. You will also find allies in this task: you will find people, like your college counselor, who reliably amplify the signal for you. You will find print or online sources that prove their worth over time and also amplify the signal. And most importantly, as you learn more about colleges and about what you are looking for in a college, your own powers of discernment will improve. Your ability to filter information will improve quickly as you go along.

Step Two: Use Multiple Sources of Information

When you're trying to learn about individual colleges, you have many resources at your disposal. From your classes in high school, you're probably familiar with the terms *primary* and *secondary* sources.

To be most efficient and effective with your college research, start with primary source materials. These will be print or online materials created by the colleges themselves as well as contact with people currently on campus, such as admissions officers, faculty, staff, and current students. Information that comes directly from the college and existing college community itself should be reliable and current. OK, mistakes do happen. Sometimes you'll get a wrong answer from an admissions officer, sometimes college websites aren't updated as quickly as they should be, and sometimes you'll run across someone whose perspective is so different from yours that his information isn't relevant, but on the whole, the primary source information should serve you well.

Once you've collected some primary source information about a college, move on to secondary sources. Secondary source information about colleges comes from everywhere other than the college itself. Among other things, secondary sources offer subjective opinions about colleges. Secondary source information about colleges is plentiful and keeps increasing. This information is often quite interesting (and sometimes sensational) but is subject to the vagaries of the opinions and attitudes of its producer. You'll find more noise in the secondary source material, so keep asking: What is the source? Why should I believe this?

Step Three: Balance Remote and Local Sources
In an op-ed for the *New York Times* from August 4, 2012, psychologist Daniel Wegner wrote:

> The line that separates my mind from the Internet is getting blurry. This has been happening ever since I realized how often it feels as though I know something just because I can find it with Google. Technically, of course, I don't know it. But when there's a smartphone or iPad in reach, I know everything the Internet knows. Or at least, that's how it feels.

When so much information about colleges is available online, it may begin to feel as though, in Wegner's terms, the "line that separates [your] mind from the Internet is getting blurry." It may feel as though you can learn everything about a school just by using what I call "remote" resources and never budging from your computer.

You can certainly make a lot of headway with your research by taking advantage of remote sources, but you will always want to balance this information with personal experience. I'm not saying that you need to visit every campus that interests you before you decide to apply, but do take advantage of the opportunities you'll have to make personal contact with an admissions officer or other individuals, including current students, faculty members, and alumni, who have direct and recent experience with the college. Through personal contact, you'll be able to pick up a lot of information about the atmosphere of a college that won't necessarily be apparent from remote sources.

See what opportunities each college presents for personal contact: Will an admissions officer be visiting your town and conducting an information session? Is there a recent graduate of the school living nearby who you can talk to? Can you Skype with a current student? If you have the time and resources to visit the campus itself, especially when classes are in session, that's ideal.

It's all about balance, really. Gathering information from remote sources is a great way to start and can be very efficient. But it will always be important to test the impressions you form remotely in the local laboratory of your real life.

Step Four: It All Comes Back to You
After you have collected information about colleges from a variety of sources and started to develop a pretty good picture of each institution on your list, your last step in the process is to figure out how closely each college matches your preferences. At this stage, everyone finds that the colleges they initially researched overlap

Gather and Evaluate Information Effectively

in varying degrees with their priorities. Some places meet almost every priority, some meet a few, and others may meet almost none. It can be helpful at this point to have a visual tool that helps you quickly see how closely each college matches your preferences. Some students like to make a spreadsheet so they have a visual representation of the matching points between each college and their personal priorities. Many students I've worked with have liked this approach. There is something about looking at the spreadsheet that really helps clarify whether or not each college is a match.

We'll get into the process of making decisions about which colleges stay on your list and which colleges get the boot in the next chapters, but before we leave info-gathering mode, I'd like you to do one last thing with your initial list of colleges: add a note (or a column, if you're using a spreadsheet) for each college that reflects the degree of overlap between your academic profile, including GPA and SAT or ACT scores, and the academic profile for students the college has recently admitted.

If your high school uses a software program like Naviance, for example, it will be easy to get this information. Just look at the scattergrams, and you can see how your profile compares to the profiles of students from your high school who have applied to that college. If your high school doesn't use Naviance or a similar type of data collection program, you can get a rough idea of the overlap by looking at the incoming student profile for the most recent entering freshman class on each college's website and comparing the GPA and test scores for admitted students with your own profile.

If your academic profile is significantly stronger than those of students recently admitted to the college, add an *L* to your notes for this college. If your profile is similar to the profiles of recently admitted students (or perhaps a little stronger), add a *P* to your notes. If your profile is weaker than the profiles of admitted students (or if any college on your list accepts 25 percent or less of applicants), add an *H* to your notes. We'll come back to these notations later in the process.

Assessing the overlap between your academic profile and the profiles of entering students at particular colleges can be tricky, so you may want to ask for help with this step. Your college counselor should be able to offer helpful information at this point, so don't hesitate to check in with her. If you don't have a college counselor to help you, you may want to look at some of the websites that offer to calculate your chances of admission to particular colleges. Remember that sites like these offer only general information, though—they do not give you an ironclad prediction of your own outcomes.

Looking Ahead
Congratulations on finishing the second step in this process. How is your list of colleges shaping up? Have you found a lot of good matches? Or are you worried that you don't have enough colleges that seem to be good matches? We'll talk about how to trim or expand your list as necessary in the next chapters.

Once they start, most students find that it is kind of fun to research colleges. The tricky thing with research, though, is knowing when to say, "Enough." One of the challenges of the college search process is coming to terms with the fact that you will never have 100 percent of the information available about any particular college. It will always be possible to consult "just one more source" or check out one more campus video recently uploaded to the web. But don't let research become a disguise for procrastination. Keep moving ahead.

We talked about this earlier, but it's worth repeating: your priorities may change and develop as you move through the stages of the admissions process. Trust yourself and your instincts as you go

Gather and Evaluate Information Effectively

along. Don't be afraid to change your mind about a college when you are presented with compelling new information or when you realize that your priorities have shifted.

Lastly, to return to the idea of signal vs. noise: because each person's starting point and priorities in a college search are different, the information that is signal for you may be noise for someone else, and vice versa. Therefore, you and your friends can reach very different conclusions about the same college or colleges.

Now that you're armed with the information you have gathered and evaluated, you are ready to move on to the next step: making choices based on this information.

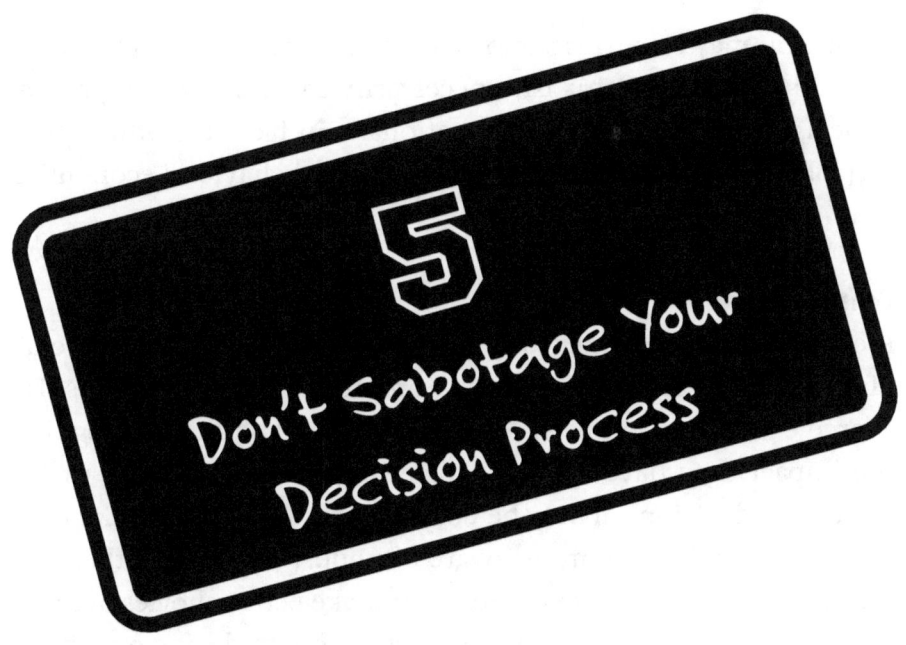

5 Don't Sabotage Your Decision Process

After setting your starting point and researching colleges, you have arrived at what many students feel to be the most challenging part of the admissions process: making decisions. From the big universe of colleges, you first have to choose a subset of schools to apply to, and then, once your results arrive, choose a college to attend. Making these decisions is often more complicated than students anticipate.

If you're like most people, you probably feel that you make decisions in a pretty straightforward and logical way—at least most of the time. When presented with a choice, you'll weigh the pros and cons, and then pick the best option, the one that has the most desirable outcome for you. This is the traditional view of how the decision-making process works, and it is based on the assumption that human beings are basically rational.

But you may be surprised to learn that an increasing amount of research shows that this isn't necessarily the case. Our approach to decision making isn't always rational—in fact, it is often "predictably irrational," to borrow a phrase from behavioral economist Dan Ariely.

What's Ahead
Professor Ariely and other social scientists have documented several of what I'll call *cognitive habits* that can influence our decisions. To a large extent, we're unaware of these habits and don't recognize the impact they have on our choices. As you get ready to make important decisions about the colleges you apply to and the college you attend, being more aware of underlying factors that can influence your decisions will help you make better choices overall. In this chapter, we'll look specifically at how to decide on a final list of colleges to apply to. In the next chapter, we'll look at how to make the decision about which college to attend.

What Are the Obstacles?
Social scientists have devoted a lot of time to investigating how and why people make the choices they do about a whole range of topics. Cognitive psychologists and behavioral economists, in particular, offer many insights that are relevant to the process of choosing colleges to apply to and attend. For now, though, I want to look at several concepts that exert the most influence on student choices.

Anchors and Herding
Professor Ariely's work illustrates the importance of anchors in the decision-making process. As behavioral economists use the term, an *anchor* is a piece of information that serves as the basis you use to compare similar items. So, for example, if you are accustomed to paying a particular price for your jar of peanut

butter, that price becomes the mental anchor you rely on when evaluating the cost of other peanut butters you might want to try.

Professor Ariely and other researchers have noted that we tend to choose our anchors locally; that is, we have a tendency to make comparisons to other objects or opportunities that are within our immediate sphere of attention.

I have observed that local anchors play a big role in a student's approach to the college selection process. Within each high school, there is usually a group of popular colleges that students apply to and enroll at year after year. The popular group of colleges varies from high school to high school, and from region to region around the country, but it is a consistent feature of the college counseling landscape.

The persistence of these popular college clusters illustrates how we share anchors with those around us and how these shared anchors can lead to similarities in the college choices within particular high schools. (Social scientists call our tendency to prefer what others in our set prefer—in this case, a group of colleges—"herding.") Current students look at the college choices of previous students to validate their own choices, and over time those choices become entrenched within a high school community. The popular group of colleges becomes the anchor group of schools to which all others are compared. The anchor group can become so fixed that when a student opts *not* to apply to any of the anchor colleges, he may be seen as weird and out of step with classmates.

Whether intentional or not, reliance on local anchors and a preference for choices made by the herd can restrict a student's view of available and acceptable college options.

Inattentional Blindness

When you start the admissions process, it's likely that you will already be aware of several colleges. These may be the anchor colleges popular in your high school, universities your family members have attended, or schools with sports teams you follow, for example. No matter how they entered your field of awareness, you have a general sense of familiarity with these colleges. This makes them comfortable choices. Because you're already aware of them, these colleges seem kind of preapproved.

As people process information, one cognitive shortcut involves equating name recognition and/or popularity with quality. Most people have a general sense that if a product or service is good, they will have heard about it. That is certainly true with colleges. The yardstick of "have I heard of it" is often employed to determine whether a specific college is a "good school."

But the habit of using your own awareness of a college as an indicator of its quality is problematic. This is where anchoring and herding, combined with what psychologists Christopher Chabris and Daniel Simons have labeled "inattentional blindness," can sabotage your decision process.

In an innovative research study called the "Invisible Gorilla" (check out the video they used in this study at: theinvisiblegorilla.com/gorilla_experiment.html), Chabris and Simons found that "we vividly experience some aspects of our world, particularly those that are the focus of our attention. But this rich experience inevitably leads to the erroneous belief that we process *all* of the detailed information around us. In essence, we know how vividly we see some aspects of our world, *but we are completely unaware of those aspects of our world that fall outside that current focus of attention*" (italics mine).

This is why you may need to push yourself to consider colleges that are less familiar within your community. This path can create more work for you. You are bound to get questions about choices unfamiliar to or viewed as unconventional by your community. I have seen this happen a lot when students apply to schools not in the anchor group at their high schools. But as students talk to people about their choices and educate others about these unfamiliar colleges, they end up making previously invisible colleges visible within their communities. That's a good thing, because it can expand the anchor group. But it can be a tiring task, always having to respond to statements like, "I haven't heard of that college. Is it a good school?" Don't forget, you always have the option of simply answering yes and moving on!

As you decide which colleges to apply to and ultimately select one to attend, go ahead and burst the bubble of inattentional blindness. *Unfamiliar* is not a synonym for *bad choice*. This is the time to stretch yourself.

TMO: Too Many Options
Stretching yourself is good, and being willing to consider colleges you haven't previously heard of is also good—to a point.

We generally believe that having options is a good thing and that having more options is preferable to having fewer. However, the research of psychologists Barry Schwartz, Sheena Iyengar, and others offers compelling evidence that this may not be so. Paradoxically, having more options can decrease one's ability to make a good decision and can decrease the satisfaction one feels with that decision. It sounds counterintuitive, but it's true: with college options, as with other things in life, it's possible to have too much of a good thing.

I frequently see students wrestling with too many options. The trajectory usually goes like this: students begin the college admissions process thinking that they will never find a college that is right for them. Then, after they begin their research, they find lots of colleges that are appealing. It's not uncommon for students to find fifteen, eighteen, or more colleges that have the qualities they seek and where they can imagine themselves being happy.

But because applying to more than eight or ten colleges takes an enormous amount of time and money (and is crazy-making for lots of other reasons too), they then are faced with paring down the list—which brings them face-to-face with what Professor Schwartz calls "the paradox of choice." As Professor Schwartz notes in his book, conveniently called *The Paradox of Choice*, "The opportunity to choose is essential for well-being, but choice has negative features, and the negative features escalate as the number of choices increases."

Several strategies can help as you evaluate options and choose a small group of colleges to apply to from a larger set of interesting possibilities. We'll explore those strategies next.

Getting Past These Obstacles
Now we get down to brass tacks with the decision process. At this point it's likely that your research has turned up a dozen or so colleges that appeal to you. Some students may have more than this, while some may have fewer.

Ultimately, you will want to apply to about ten colleges.

Why this number? Over the years, I have found that this is what makes the most sense for students in terms of the time, effort, and cost involved. You want to make the best possible presentation with each application, and if you apply to more than about ten schools, it becomes very hard to do this. I've also found that applying to about ten carefully chosen colleges usually allows students to have options in the spring after decision letters are received. (The operative phrase in that previous sentence is *carefully chosen*.)

How do you whittle a large list of appealing colleges down to the group of ten or so that you will apply to?

Step One: Review Your Position
What does your current list of "colleges that interest me" look like?

If you have made a spreadsheet or other list that enables you to quickly see how each college on the list does or doesn't meet your preferences, it should be pretty easy for you to go through and pull out the colleges that best match up with your priorities. Eliminate the colleges with fewer of the qualities you seek from your list.

Step Two: Calibrate

In the previous chapter, I asked you to make a note about the degree of overlap between your academic profile and the academic profiles of students admitted to the colleges you're considering. This is where that information comes in handy. With your newly trimmed list of colleges in front of you, circle or transcribe the *L*, *P*, or *H* next to each college on the list.

The traditional wisdom in assembling lists of colleges to apply to is that you will want a few in the *H* (for highly competitive) category. These are schools you like but where the academic profile of admitted students is stronger than your profile, and/or schools you like but which admit fewer than 25 percent of applicants. Even if you have straight A's and perfect SAT or ACT scores, put an *H* next to any colleges on your list that admit fewer than 25 percent of their applicants. These schools turn away many students with perfect academic profiles each year.

Then you will want to include a few schools in the *P* (for possibility) category. These are schools you like where the academic profile of admitted students is pretty similar to your own. The last few spots on the list of colleges you'll apply to goes to schools you have marked with an *L* (for likely). These are colleges where your academic profile is stronger than that of most admitted students. Using that formula, your final list of colleges might include three *H* schools, three *P* schools, and three *L* schools.

However, that's just the traditional wisdom. It may be that you don't want to apply to any colleges in the *H* category, which is fine.

Your final list might include three *P* schools and four *L* schools. Or you might decide on five *H* schools and four *L* schools. You can mix this up in any number of ways, but you will always want to include at least three *L* schools on your final list.

Time Out: Exceptions
The strategy I've laid out here will be appropriate for the majority of students who plan to apply to college using a regular decision program. This strategy is also appropriate for students who want to apply to a college using some type of early application program. You may have one super-favorite college that you'll apply to for early decision, or to which you may want to submit an early action application, but you'll still have to have a list of other colleges to apply to, just in case that early decision or early action application is deferred or denied.

What if the college or colleges that most interest you all happen to fall in the *L* category? Do you still need to apply to eight to ten of those?

If you are in this position, I'd say that you don't have to push yourself to apply to eight colleges. But apply to at least three or four of the *L* category colleges that interest you. This is especially important if you are applying for financial aid—you will want to have the opportunity to compare financial aid offers at a few places before making a final choice about which college to attend. Second, as you begin your senior year, even if you are completely in love with one college that looks like a clear *L*, it makes sense to apply to at least two other *L* colleges. You might change your mind about your priorities during your senior year. I have seen this happen to students a number of times—while they assured me in November that there was no way they'd change their minds about a particular college, come spring they were happy to have another option or two. (This is why I'm not a fan of binding early decision programs. A lot happens during senior year that changes students' perspectives on themselves and their priorities, and it is not at all uncommon for students who loved a college enough to commit to it in the fall to find they have second thoughts and regret that commitment later.)

Step Three: Fold in the Financials

In addition to calibrating your colleges academically, you will want to do this financially too. If you have applied for any type of financial aid, be it need-based aid or merit scholarships, you should receive notification about aid awards right around the time you receive an offer of admission. In most cases, you won't have the full information about college costs for your first year of enrollment until late in the admissions cycle.

However, there are tools available that can help you get a rough estimate of what it may cost you to attend a particular college. The College Board (collegeboard.org) and FinAid (finaid.org) websites have financial information and various calculators that many students and parents find helpful. You can also look for the "net price calculator" on the websites of the colleges that interest you.

Once you have an estimate of costs for each college on your list, sit down and go over this information with your parents. You should have had a preliminary conversation with them early in the process, when you were setting your starting point, but now is the time to look at the actual numbers. This is the time to figure out if the costs of any particular college on your list are out of reach for your family. If so, you may want to delete that college from your list, or at least give it an asterisk to indicate that even if you are admitted, it may not be financially possible for you to attend the school. And then make sure you have several other colleges on your list that are academically *and* financially likely for you.

Given the uncertain economic climate, I advise all of the students I work with to include at least one in-state public university on the final list of colleges they apply to, no matter what their family's financial circumstances. You never know what might happen between the time you apply to college and the spring of your senior year, and it just makes sense to have at least one lower-cost public college or university on your list.

Step Four: Pulling It All Together
Once you have completed the steps above and created your list of colleges to apply to, you're almost finished. Now, with the list in front of you, ask yourself these questions about each college on the list:

- If this is the only college I'm admitted to, will I be happy going to school there?
- Am I applying to this college for me or to please someone else?

Make any necessary changes to the list based on your responses and then look at the whole thing again. Ask two more questions:

- Is my list the right size for me?
- Should I pare it down a little more or add a few more schools?

If your list is too large, it may help to have your college counselor or an adult who knows you but who doesn't have a stake in your college choices go over it with you. (So choose someone other than a parent.) It's often helpful to talk about the process through which you made each choice with someone, since this forces you to look at your reasoning each step of the way.

On the Other Hand...

If your list is too small and you're having trouble finding other colleges that appeal to you, that could mean that your expectations are too high and you're looking for perfect matches. It's not likely that a college will meet each one of your priorities 100 percent, but you will still have a wonderful experience at colleges that match most of your priorities 80 percent. Push yourself to expand your horizons.

If seeking perfection is not the problem and you still can't find enough colleges that appeal to you, ask yourself this hard question: Do I really want to go to college right away?

Sometimes students who have a difficult time finding the right colleges to apply to just aren't ready for college—for a variety of reasons. If this is how you're feeling, you may want to explore the possibility of taking time off after high school to work, volunteer, or participate in an established gap-year program. You may want to postpone the question of college for now. If so, I will tell you that getting off the educational conveyor belt requires courage, since it is an unconventional choice, but I have seen students benefit enormously from taking time off before going to college.

If you (and your parents) decide that going to college right after high school isn't the right choice, you should talk with the college counselor or guidance counselor at your high school to let them know this is what you've decided. You can also get information about how to contact your school counselors and any teachers you might need to write recommendations for you if you apply to college at some point in the future. You might be advised to submit a few college applications while you are a senior anyway so that you may have the option of deferring your entry to college for a year.

6
More about Making Good Decisions

Well, here you are at last: about to complete your admissions process and choose a college to attend. Let's get started!

What's Ahead

If you have only one option for college, either because you applied to a college under a binding early decision plan and were admitted or because you hold one offer of admission from the group of colleges you applied to, you're done.

Congratulations!

If you followed all the steps I outlined and carefully chose the colleges you applied to, I'll assume this college matches your preferences and is one where you can see yourself being happy. Nice work! If you are required to submit an enrollment deposit, go ahead and do that well before its stated deadline, and then celebrate.

If you have two or more offers of admission from colleges that you like equally, you have more work to do.

What Are the Obstacles?

Making that final choice—saying yes to one school and no to others—can be pretty difficult. Anchoring and herding, inattentional blindness, and having too many options also influence this final stage of the process, and there are other factors that can sabotage your final choice as well. We will look at those potential obstacles and then discuss strategies to avoid them.

The Challenge of Commitment

Life is all about choices, and you have made a whole bunch of decisions that have brought you to this juncture. So we know you can make decisions for yourself! However, for most students, choosing which college to attend is the most significant and high-stakes choice they have ever made, and that's scary.

The other thing is that, assuming you were thoughtful about choosing the colleges you applied to, the colleges that admitted you all match up well with your priorities. You might feel as though committing to one college is hard because your options are equally appealing.

So you're stuck.

You're not alone, though. Professor Ariely's research has shown we often "cannot stand the idea of closing the doors on our alternatives." In fact, we dislike the idea of loss so much that we will devote a lot of energy to keeping our options open. We often overlook the cost in time and energy, among other things, of trying to maintain multiple opportunities. We'll come back to this point in a minute.

More about Making Good Decisions

The Myth of the Perfect Match

You may have difficulty picking one college to attend because you feel that there is one perfect match for you. With a little more time or a little more information, you tell yourself, you'll figure out which one that is.

This is a potent myth, but a myth, nonetheless. As I discussed at the beginning of the book, there are a number of colleges at which you can be happy and successful. You proved that through the research you did when choosing colleges to apply to. So trust yourself now, trust your research, and keep it in mind as we move on to next steps.

Accepting Uncertainty

This is easier said than done. Ultimately, your choice of college is going to be a leap of faith. You've done a lot of research, but it's impossible to predict exactly how your experience will unfold at any college you choose. Coming face-to-face with uncertainty is as difficult at this stage of the admissions process as it was when you applied to schools, when you couldn't know for sure what the results would be. Do now as you did then: keep moving forward and trust the process.

Getting Past These Obstacles

Simply being aware of the cognitive habits that can influence your decisions gives you a giant advantage as you make the choice of a college to attend.

Knowing about anchoring and herding will help you guard against choosing a college just because it is a favorite option for students from your high school.

Understanding that having more options won't guarantee greater satisfaction with a particular decision can help you limit the field from which your choice will be made.

Knowing that closing doors on alternatives is difficult for everyone and that there is no perfect college out there can relieve you of some of the stress involved with making a choice.

Finally, remembering that you have accomplished a lot already and made good choices that have gotten you to this point should give you confidence as you choose the college you will attend.

So much for the big picture. Here are a few strategies to help you sort through your options.

Step One: Revisit Your Starting Point

Are the priorities you started with the same priorities you have now? Be honest with yourself. If your feelings have changed, take those changes into account as you compare your options. Try not to judge those changes, because that will ultimately be unproductive. Your goal is, as it always was, to have as clear a view as possible of the priorities, expectations, and assumptions you bring to the table. Accept any changes in your thinking and move on.

Step Two: Gather Any Last Information You Need

Do you need any additional information in order to make a final choice? Perhaps you are waiting to hear about a financial aid award, or perhaps you want to visit a campus, for example. If you need more information, figure out how to get that as quickly as possible, because the clock is ticking. May 1 is the typical deadline to accept or decline an offer of admission. Remember that once you are an admitted student, college admissions officers will want to see you enroll at their institutions, so don't hesitate to contact admissions officers if and when you need help gathering more information.

Step Three: Pay Attention to Your Inner Voice

If you don't need more information to make this choice, then what is your heart telling you? Is there a place where you just feel that you'll be happiest? You may not be able to articulate why, but honor your intuition as you make a choice.

If you are having trouble hearing your inner voice, try this exercise, which many students have found helpful. Take a full day to imagine yourself at each college you're considering. Think about which residence hall you'd like to live in, pick out classes you'd like to take, and imagine, in as much detail as possible, what it would be like for you to attend that one college. Think only about this one college and note how you feel throughout the day as you imagine that this is where you've decided to go. Repeat this exercise as many times as necessary for you to compare the different colleges you're considering. Pay attention to how you feel on each day as you imagine yourself attending that college. It's likely that when you're finished with this exercise, one college will simply feel most right to you.

One other thing that can help you hear your inner voice is to stake out some quiet space for yourself. Take a day or two or three. Let family and friends know that you are fully engaged with the decision process and that you're at a point where outside opinions are no longer useful. Take the topic of college off the table for discussion and give yourself time to think things over without the "benefit" of extra input.

Step Four: Give Yourself a Deadline
Taking more time to make a decision isn't going to make the process easier. Trust me on this—when students push the final decision to the last possible moment, they only end up lengthening the amount of time they feel stressed. So once you have the information you need to make your decision, set a deadline at least a few days before your enrollment deposit is due. Regard that deadline as nonnegotiable and take any action you need to confirm your decision with the college on or before that date.

Setting and adhering to a relatively short timeline for your decision process can be the single most helpful step you can take to reduce stress.

As noted previously, closing doors is difficult for everyone. Taking more time to consider, reconsider, and worry about what each doorway holds is only going to complicate the process of saying yes to one college and no to others.

Step Five: Make the Decision and Move On

Don't spend time second-guessing yourself. Once you've made the decision and confirmed your enrollment with the college of your choice, get on with the rest of your life! As Professor Schwartz notes in *The Paradox of Choice*, "When we can change our minds about our decisions, we are less satisfied with them. When a decision is final, we engage in a variety of psychological processes that enhance our feelings about the choice we made relative to the alternatives." So once you have made your choice, relax, celebrate, and enjoy the last few weeks of your senior year in high school.

And that's it! Congratulations! You have decided where you're going to go to college!

As You Look Ahead

Many of the students I work with say that after they make a final decision about which college to attend, they feel as though a weight has been lifted from their shoulders. Don't be surprised if you feel that way too. College has been close to the center of your attention continuously for the past several months, and now that this process has concluded, you have the time and freedom to turn your attention to other things.

It's not uncommon, though, for students to feel a little bit at sea as the process concludes. This is also not surprising. It takes

More about Making Good Decisions

some time to readjust when something that has been at the center of your life is no longer there.

If you are like many of the students I work with, your feelings are kind of jumbled at this point. You feel happy that the college admissions process is behind you, but you may also feel a little sad and nostalgic about the fact that your time in high school is coming to an end. You're excited about the next stage of your life and the opportunities that college will bring but uncertain about what lies ahead and how you will manage the transition, academically and/or socially. You're enthusiastic about being in a new environment and meeting new people, but wondering if and how you'll maintain your high school friendships. And you may have lingering thoughts about whether or not you made the right decision.

You should acknowledge those feelings, but don't let them get in the way. If you keep focusing on the past, it will be harder for you to see the many exciting opportunities that lie ahead. And it may be helpful for you to know that the vast majority of students, once enrolled at a college, can't imagine being as happy anywhere but there.

Because the truth is, like Dorothy in *The Wizard of Oz*, you already have the heart, courage, and brains you need for success in college. Use those qualities and don't let your doubts—or whatever form your own personal Wicked Witch takes—get in the way.

Best of luck to you!

7
For Parents

I mentioned in Chapter 3 that as I begin my work with students, I ask how they're feeling about the college process and if they have questions or concerns as they look ahead. I also ask if there is anything they wish they could tell their parents as the process gets underway. Here are a few representative responses to that last question:

- "I know my parents have high expectations. I'm worried about letting them down."
- "I know my parents will be proud of me no matter what, and I appreciate their continuing support. But I don't need them to hound me."
- "Parents should advise their children, not drive/control them."

COLLEGE ADMISSIONS without the Crazy

Moving Beyond *We're* Applying to College
It is endlessly fascinating to me to see how students' ideas about themselves, their abilities, and what they want for the future can change during that period of about eighteen months from the second semester of junior year through high school graduation. Beyond the nuts and bolts of researching, applying to, and ultimately choosing a college to attend, the admissions process is a developmental milestone for many students. It is an intense time for teenagers, one in which they are challenged to apply cognitive skills in a new arena and to develop confidence in themselves and their paths. It is also a time for students to build their resilience muscles.

There is much about this process that is challenging for parents too. Of course you want the best for your child. But here's the rub: you and your child may disagree about what's best. Moreover, you may have very different ideas about the means through which the designated best is to be achieved. You may also have different ideas about how much assistance your child needs as he works toward that goal.

One very experienced school head I know talked about the parent-child dynamic in the teenage years this way: the objective, as he saw it, was for parents to move from a management to a consulting role in the child's life—without getting fired along the way.

That's a very apt way to think about the task. However, technology has complicated this transition by making it easier for parents to stay involved in managing the details of a child's life. In her book *Alone Together*, MIT professor Sherry Turkle makes the point that technology (the cell phone, in particular) tethers parents and children in ways not previously possible. Turkle also believes that our networked culture has incurred a shift in our ideas about psychological autonomy. Commenting on behavior she sees in her students—such as texting parents multiple times each day for input and advice about even the smallest of issues—she notes that this lack of separation from the parents would have appeared as a pathology twenty years ago but now isn't perceived as at all unusual.

We're all adjusting to these new levels of technologically enhanced connection and finding that there are positive aspects, certainly. But parents do need to be aware of the ways in which this constant connection can undermine a child's sense of independence and ownership of the admissions process.

So what's a parent to do? How can you strike a balance between loving support and appropriate supervision while at the same time letting your child drive the bus and take full advantage of the unique learning opportunity the college admissions process presents?

Over the years I've seen parents and children navigate this process smoothly, not so smoothly, and with levels of anger, anxiety, and conflict that left me wondering if their relationships would be permanently scarred. Every family is different, and every family brings its own aspirations, fears, communication styles, and ways of expressing love and concern to the college admissions table. This means, unfortunately, that there isn't a one-size-fits-all prescription for success in this process. What works well for some families may be ineffective and inappropriate for others.

Secrets of Successful Families

But before you despair, I can tell you that families who emerge from the admissions process in good shape do have certain traits in common.

First, they approach the admissions process as a partnership in which the child plays the lead role. Forging this partnership doesn't mean that the student calls all the shots or has absolute veto power in every instance. It's more a matter of agreeing that everyone has a role to play and being clear about those roles. Everyone has ideas, preferences, and skills to contribute. It's also important to acknowledge that although the student is driving the bus, both driver and passengers may suffer unpleasant consequences if the rules of the road are ignored.

Second, as far as possible, each member of the partnership puts his or her expectations and assumptions on the table as the process gets underway. As you discuss expectations and assumptions, it's important to be honest about who is going to do what and when. Who will research colleges? Schedule campus visits? Make travel arrangements for campus visit trips away from home? Arrange interviews? Who will have access to a student's online applications and communications from colleges? Who will submit the applications, and when will applications be submitted? ("Before the deadline" isn't specific enough as an answer, by the way.) Who will be involved with writing and editing the essay? What role will the school counselor play? Will an independent college consultant be part of the process?

Discussing the financial realities of the admissions process and college costs is challenging for many families, regardless of whether funds are already available for college. But it is important for the student to know at the outset if, for example, the final college choice will hinge primarily on the financial aid packages received or if she will be expected to pay for a portion of the application expenses or college costs by holding a summer job or a work-study job on campus.

I have seen firsthand that it is crushing for a child to begin the process believing that the family has the financial side of things covered, regardless of any aid awards, and then discover a few weeks before the final enrollment decision is to be made that this wasn't the case. I know it can be difficult, but it's much better for all involved to have an honest discussion about finances at the beginning of this process.

Third, the family puts boundaries around the admissions process so that it doesn't become the sole focus of the child's senior year. They also develop a plan for checking in with each other throughout the process. Putting a fence around the topic of college admissions helps keep the process in perspective and also helps students avoid feeling ambushed by questions about their college research and the status of their applications. If students know that they are expected to discuss their plans and progress at a specific time each week, they can be prepared—the topic comes up for discussion, it's discussed, and then it's tabled until the next time. Of course questions and comments may arise in between planned discussions, but those are dealt with as one-offs and don't automatically lead to hours of conversation about everything connected with the college process. So a simple question like, "Do you think I should take the SAT in January or March?" shouldn't open the door to an hours-long airing of all things college.

Last, and most importantly, families who navigate this process successfully recognize that there are bound to be glitches along the way. Very few things in life go exactly according to plan, and the college admissions process is no exception. Glitches happen.

Along the road to college, each student begins the transition from "kid world" to "adult world." That transition can be tricky to navigate. These two worlds can seem similar but are actually quite different. For example, words like *now* and *deadline* have different meanings in kid world than they do in adult world. This can lead to familial friction. And as adults, it is easy to forget that our greater life experience enables us to filter information and make decisions more quickly than teenagers can. This may lead students and parents to be impatient with or intolerant of their different information-gathering styles and the criteria and timetables they use to reach decisions. When these situations arise, it can be helpful to think of them as examples of culture clash, not personal attacks.

Do You Need Outside Help?

The question of whether or not to work with an independent college consultant can be difficult to answer.

On the upside, an experienced and qualified independent counselor can provide a useful perspective to students and parents, especially in cases where college counseling resources at a student's high school are limited. An outside counselor can also be a helpful buffer if family dynamics are such that most discussions about college deteriorate into shouting matches or sullen silence. Finally, some families just feel more comfortable knowing that they have another perspective in the mix—someone outside the high school that they can talk to.

On the downside, an inexperienced independent counselor may do more harm than good. He may offer incomplete or incorrect information to the family or interfere with the work the high school's college counselor is doing on behalf of a student. Some students also view the hiring of an independent counselor as embarrassing training wheels—the action of parents who lack confidence in their child's ability to accomplish goals without assistance.

If you do decide to go this route, be sure to do your homework so you find a counselor who is experienced and ethical. Websites for the professional college admissions and college counseling organizations all have good information about how to find an independent counselor—they are good places to begin your search. I have included URLs for these organizations in Appendix 2.

Ultimately, the goal for parents throughout the admissions process is to model the behavior you want to see in your child. Stop and reflect for a moment: How do you talk about the admissions process and share information (or not!) about how other students and parents are handling things? How are you managing your own stress? How are you dealing with setbacks? Remember that in the admissions process, as in everything else, your child will be watching and taking cues from you along the way.

If you're used to being the manager of your child's life, it will be challenging to move into a consulting role. Stepping in may be second nature for you, so you'll have to practice stepping back. It can be scary, but it's totally doable, as the families with whom I have worked can attest.

If you need a mantra to help get you through, remember that great British slogan, "Keep calm and carry on."

Acknowledgments

College Admissions Without the Crazy got its start as a blog. Some of the material in this book originally appeared in my blog, Admissions Café (admissionscafe.wordpress.com). Many friends and colleagues on both sides of the admissions desk were kind enough to read and comment on my posts and offer encouragement as the idea for this book took shape. Thanks especially to Blythe Butler, Sue Phillips, Laura Sellers, and Sharon Ivey, who read and discussed portions of the book, and offered useful questions and feedback.

Phyllis Supple deserves a special award as "beta-reader extraordinaire." Her insights about the admissions process and the way it is experienced by students were enormously helpful.

Thanks are due also to the talented folks at Indigo Editing who helped transform the pages of text into a real book. Kristen Hall-Geisler, Ali McCart, and Susan DeFreitas provided careful and professional editing and proofreading, for which I am very grateful. And I shudder to think what the final product might have looked like without the creativity and design expertise of Vinnie Kinsella. Thank you!

Over the years, I have had the good fortune to work with many talented and dedicated people in admissions and college counseling offices all over the world. I can't possibly list each one, but I thank them for inspiring me, teaching me, travelling with me, and making the long hours of work memorable in so many ways.

Appendix 1: Questionnaire

INSTRUCTIONS: Find some time when you can be alone and uninterrupted to answer the following questions. You may discuss your answers with anyone you like later on, but for now we're after your opinions, uninfluenced by others.

Think carefully about your responses to the questions ahead but don't agonize over them. There are no right or wrong answers; this exercise is about discovering what you think and what you prefer. You can work through these questions in any order and return to complete or change your responses later.

Last but not least, it is important to keep a record of your answers, either on paper or as a file on your computer. You will return to these responses periodically throughout the admissions process, and they will be especially useful when you are making a final choice about which college to attend.

A. Academics/Life in High School

1. What do you like most about your high school? What do you like least?
2. What are your favorite subjects? (Focus on the subject area itself and separate that from your feelings about the teachers who have taught those subjects.)
3. Do you want to continue to study any of these subjects in college? What other subjects do you think you might want to study in college? (Not necessarily as a major; I'm looking here for areas you simply want to learn more about.)
4. Who are your favorite teachers? Why? What makes them stand out?
5. About how many people are in each of your individual

classes? (How many take math, English, or other academic classes with you?) Would you prefer larger or smaller classes?
6. Are most of your classes *seminar style* (where students and teachers discuss the topics and there is lots of time for questions), *lecture style* (where the teacher presents information to the class and where there may be limited time for questions), or *lab style* (where students are split into small groups and work together to investigate questions)? Which style or styles do you like most? Is there a style that you really don't like at all?
7. Is there any course, activity, or sport that you wanted to pursue in high school but couldn't? (Perhaps you didn't have time, or the course, activity, or sport wasn't offered.)
8. What do the majority of students from your high school do after graduation? Of the group of graduates that goes on to college, which colleges do they usually attend? Does your school place a lot of emphasis on where graduates go to college?
9. What colleges are your friends considering?
10. Are there any events or circumstances from your high school years that you might need to explain in an application? For example, have you attended more than one high school? Did you have an illness or accident that affected your grades? Have you been subject to any disciplinary actions?

B. You and Your Work Style
1. What clubs, activities, and/or sports are important to you? Do you think you might like to continue with any of these in college?
2. Do you have an outstanding talent in any area (including but not limited to: athletics, music, science, debate, art, or leadership)?

Appendix 1: Questionnaire

3. Does religion play an important role in your life? Do you think you might like to attend a college affiliated with a particular religion?
4. Do you think you want to stay close to home for college, or are you interested in looking at schools that are farther away? Is it important to you to be close to or in a city, or can you see yourself being happy in a suburban or rural location?
5. Is it important to you to go to a college that is well-known?
6. When you are given an assignment, do you like to have a clear set of instructions or guidelines, or do you enjoy figuring things out for yourself?
7. Do you enjoy working on assignments or problems as part of a group, or would you rather work alone?
8. How important is it for you to be able to connect with your teachers, to see them individually and ask questions or discuss topics from class?
9. Do you have difficulty learning any particular subjects, or have you been diagnosed with a learning disability?
10. Do you enjoy being in an environment where people are very competitive academically and very aware of their grades?

C. Family Environment and Expectations
1. Will you be the first person in your family to go to college?
2. Do you think your family expects you to go to a particular college or type of college? Does your family feel that it is important for you to attend a college that is well-known?
3. Does your family prefer that you stay closer to home for college, or is location not a concern?
4. Is there a college that several of your family members have attended? Is there an expectation that you will apply to this college?

5. Do you have siblings whose college choices or plans factor into your thinking?
6. How are your parents feeling about your college applications process?
7. How much do you want to involve your parents in your college applications process?
8. What do you know about how your education will be paid for? Has your family set aside any money for your education?
9. Will you want to or need to apply for scholarships or loans, or hold jobs to help pay for college?
10. Do you think that you might go on to graduate or professional school after college?

As I mentioned before, there are no right or wrong answers to these questions. They are intended to get you thinking about the variety of characteristics and qualities you prefer in your academic and social environments so you can use these to guide your college search. These questions are also intended to help you gain a sense of the assumptions and expectations that you (and the many groups of which you are a part) hold as you enter the college search.

Appendix 2: Resources

For college research:
  ACT: www.actstudent.org
  The College Board: www.collegeboard.org and
    www.bigfuture.collegeboard.org
  College Navigator: www.nces.ed.gov/collegenavigator
  Cappex: www.cappex.com
  Zinch: www.zinch.com

For information about financial aid and college costs:
  Federal Student Aid: www.studentaid.ed.gov
  The Smart Student Guide to Financial Aid: www.finaid.org

For general information about the college admissions process:
  National Association for College Admission Counseling:
    www.nacacnet.org

For information about independent college counselors:
  Higher Education Consultants Association: www.hecaonline.org
  Independent Education Consultants Association:
    www.iecaonline.com

Books cited:
  Alone Together, by Sherry Turkle
  The Art of Choosing, by Sheena Iyengar
  The Invisible Gorilla, by Christopher Chabris and Daniel Simons
  The Paradox of Choice, by Barry Schwartz
  Predictably Irrational, by Dan Ariely
  The Signal and the Noise, by Nate Silver

About the Author

Nancy Donehower, Ph.D., has over thirty years of experience in the college admissions field. Her unique perspective on the admissions process is informed by her background as a psychologist and by her work in high schools and colleges across the country. She has been an admissions dean at highly selective colleges on both coasts (Sarah Lawrence College, Duke University, and Reed College) and the director of college counseling at two rigorous college preparatory high schools. She is currently an educational consultant in private practice. Nancy has taught popular workshops and lectured about aspects of the admissions process to students and families in the United States and abroad. Her articles and commentaries about college admissions have appeared in several publications and on public radio.

The College Admissions Without the Crazy series:

College Admissions Without the Crazy

College Application Essays Without the Crazy
(e-book)

Start Your College Search Without the Crazy
(e-book, available in mid-2015)

www.ingramcontent.com/pod-product-compliance
Lightning Source LLC
Chambersburg PA
CBHW050605300426
44112CB00013B/2074